GREEN MATTERS™

Making Good Choices About
NONRENEWABLE RESOURCES

PAULA JOHANSON

rosen publishing's
rosen
central

New York

For the ones whose resources are always renewing: Erica and John

Published in 2010 by The Rosen Publishing Group, Inc.
29 East 21st Street, New York, NY 10010

Copyright © 2010 by The Rosen Publishing Group, Inc.

First Edition

Library of Congress Cataloging-in-Publication Data

Johanson, Paula.
Making good choices about nonrenewable resources / Paula Johanson.—1st ed.
    p. cm.—(Green matters)
Includes bibliographical references and index.
ISBN-13: 978-1-4358-5311-9 (library binding)
ISBN-13: 978-1-4358-5604-2 (pbk)
ISBN-13: 978-1-4358-5605-9 (6 pack)
1. Nonrenewable natural resources. 2. Natural resources. I. Title.
HC85.J64 2010
333.7—dc22

                                             2008055409

Manufactured in Malaysia

CONTENTS

INTRODUCTION

Humans have always used natural resources to change the world around them. No one knows how long ago it was that people first began to use anything that came to hand. The first kinds of tools were probably a sharp stick to dig for roots, an animal fur to keep warm in the winter, and a pile of dry grass to cushion a baby's cradle. The oldest signs and tools left by people living long ago are rocks. These rocks fit into someone's hand and were broken to have a sharp edge. People living today can trace the scratches made with these rocks on stone and bone.

The humans who are living today are changing the world around them. Modern people are leaving signs that will be visible in the future. The longest-lasting signs and tools that people living today will leave for the future are the products they are making from rocks. The rocks and mineral deposits that people find most useful are metals, fossil fuels, and radioactive materials. These minerals are being found and used at a greedy rate. In 2007, the United States alone used 20,680,000 barrels of petroleum per day, out of a total of 83,607,000 barrels used every day by countries around the world. At this rate of usage, there is only enough petroleum to last fifty years at the most, according to the U.S. Energy Information Administration and the International Energy Agency.

The signs being left behind by people living today will last longer than the Egyptian stone statue called the Great Sphinx of Giza, which is ten thousand or more years old. But the signs being left behind will not be whole works of art in twenty thousand years. The Statue of Liberty and the Golden Gate Bridge will be crumbles of corroded

metal. Burnt fossil fuels put poison traces in the air and oceans that will still cause lung and heart illnesses and cancer in the future. Radioactive waste is buried and hidden because it will still be dangerous.

Some of the earth's natural resources are renewable, such as plants and animals. Water is a resource that has a renewing cycle, as it falls from the air, runs into the oceans, and evaporates back into the air again. Rocks and mineral deposits do not grow like plants or animals. They are nonrenewable. There are only so many of them. Once humans have dug them up and used them, there are no more.

CHAPTER ①

Energy from Nonrenewable Resources

Many of the earth's natural resources are minerals. These useful rocks are nonrenewable resources. Geologists study the rock formations on and under the surface of the earth, learning about the minerals that can be found. People make mines, digging into mountains or deep into the ground. They look for ores to make metal, or stone that is good for making concrete and buildings. Another reason for mining and drilling holes deep into the ground is to find mineral deposits that can be burned.

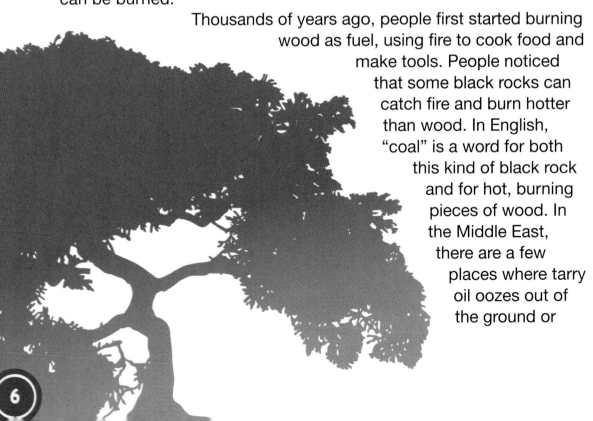

Thousands of years ago, people first started burning wood as fuel, using fire to cook food and make tools. People noticed that some black rocks can catch fire and burn hotter than wood. In English, "coal" is a word for both this kind of black rock and for hot, burning pieces of wood. In the Middle East, there are a few places where tarry oil oozes out of the ground or

The Fires of Chimera are a popular tourist destination on a mountainside near Çirali in Turkey. These natural gas fires have burned in various places since ancient times.

floats to the top of a lake. This is petroleum, from the Greek word for rock oil. Lightning striking the ground can start fires in coal beds and petroleum. In Turkey, near the village of Çirali, natural gas seeps up through cracks in the ground and bursts into flame. People learned to use whatever fuel was available, especially where there are few trees for wood.

There are uses for fire besides getting heat to cook food or smelting metals out of ores. Fuels are burned not only for heating something directly. They are also burned to use the heat to move a machine.

Hot air rises. Hot water rises, too. The heat from a fire can be used to move water in a tank and pipes. The moving water can turn the

Coal is mined from great layers that were formed millions of years ago. Strip mines remove hundreds of tons of rock to get at the coal, permanently changing an area.

blades of a fan or turbine, just like the blades of a windmill turn on a windy day. Once the turbine is turning, it can turn an electric generator. The generator makes electricity.

Another way that burning fuel is used to move a machine is in an internal combustion engine, such as the engine in most cars and trucks. The fuel burns inside the engine, making small, controlled explosions of hot gases. The hot gases push the moving parts of the engine.

If you've ever turned an eggbeater by hand or paddled a boat, you know that it takes a lot of energy to move objects around. Riding a bicycle takes some work. It is much harder to use bike pedals to try to move a large, heavy load. Many inventors have made machines that use burning fuels as a source of energy to do work. These fuels are a good source of energy. There are two kinds of

Nuclear power plants use radioactivity to heat water to turn turbines generating electricity. The cooling towers look like they're releasing smoke, but it is really clouds of steam and gases.

energy sources from nonrenewable resources: fossil fuels and radioactive energy sources.

FOSSIL FUELS

The word "fossil" is from the Latin word *fossilis*, for something that has been dug up out of the ground. A fossil is a trace in stone of something that was once living. Over thousands and millions of years, mud and sand can harden into stone and show traces of plants and animals that lived long ago. The traces could be bones from a dinosaur. They could be marks left in mud when leaves fell from trees and plants. A fossil could even be a track of footprints left by an animal running across a riverbank.

The term "fossil fuels" is used for mineral deposits like crude oil or petroleum, natural gas, and coal. Coal is a solid fuel, crude oil is a liquid fuel, and natural gas is a gaseous fuel. Each of these mineral deposits can be burned as fuel, and it is found by digging or drilling in the ground.

These mineral deposits are believed by most geologists to be formed from plants and animals that were buried hundreds of millions of years ago. In time, mud and rock covering the organic layer would cause heat and pressure. Natural gas and crude oil are the remains of ocean life like plankton and algae. Coal is the remains of ancient swamps and forests. There are a few scientists, such as Thomas Gold, who believe that these fossil fuels were not organic. Gold believes that when the planets of the solar system formed, the earth had a great deal of oil-bearing rock deep around its core. Even if that theory was correct, most of that fossil fuel would be far too deep ever to be used. Only a small amount of oil and gas has come upward through cracks, where people can find it.

Peat is also considered a fossil fuel. It is not millions of years old, though. Most peat forms in bogs. Over a few thousand years, marsh plants gradually build up and compress into peat. People use spades

Used nuclear fuel is still dangerously radioactive. This facility at Yucca Mountain in Nevada is designed to be the world's largest repository for sealed containers of nuclear waste.

to dig up blocks of peat. When any remaining water has drained out of the blocks, peat can be burned like sticks of firewood. Household stoves and fireplaces in northern Europe used up most of the peat bogs. Since the invention of furnaces that use oil, gas, or electricity, peat is used mostly in gardening as fertilizer.

RADIOACTIVE ENERGY SOURCES

There are other minerals that only have been found to be useful since the end of the nineteenth century. Pitchblende, an ore of metal that is heavier than lead, can be found in granite rocks, too. It is a source of uranium. Many chemists, such as Marie and Pierre Curie and Ernest Rutherford, studied uranium and other elements that they found in pitchblende. These studies revealed much about the way matter is made. Atoms of uranium and some other elements release particles that radiate out and interact with other atoms nearby. Marie Curie named this action radioactivity.

Curie observed an interesting quality about radioactive elements like radium. If you get enough of the radioactive element in a lump, it is warmer than its surroundings. In an hour, 1 gram (0.035 of an ounce) of radium can melt its own weight in ice. The radioactivity causes heat. The core of the earth is hot from the heat made by radioactive elements more than four and a half billion years ago.

This heat can be useful. In 1942, Enrico Fermi was the first to make what he called an atomic pile. When a pile is carefully made of pellets of uranium formed into rods, separated by control rods of carbon, the radiation increases to a critical point. Carbon rods can be removed or inserted to control the nuclear reaction. The radiation can be used to change atoms within the pile to other elements. The heat of the reaction can be used if the pile is submerged in water.

A modern nuclear reactor in an electrical power plant uses a critical mass of uranium pellets to heat water. The hot water is then used to turn turbines for electric generators. Smaller nuclear reactors with a different design are installed in submarines and large ships to generate electricity. Several space probes, such as *Galileo* and *Cassini*, have cameras and radios powered with small nuclear reactors.

The uranium fuel in a nuclear power plant is effective for only a while. Then, it needs to be removed and replaced. So do the carbon rods and other parts of the reactor. The spent fuel rods will remain radioactive for tens of thousands of years. The radiation is dangerous, causing harmful changes to body cells in living organisms. There is temporary storage for spent fuel rods near most nuclear reactors, in carefully maintained pools of water and boric acid. Reinforced concrete bunkers are also used.

A permanent way to store spent fuel rods is being designed. Sealed containers of spent fuel rods will be buried more than 1,500 feet (450 meters) underground. Geologists are selecting storage sites that have little or no groundwater. There should also be no active earthquake faults. In the United States, a site has been selected at Yucca Mountain, in an isolated part of Nevada, for use in 2010.

OTHER ENERGY SOURCES

There are other energy sources besides generators run on fossil fuels and radioactive materials. Solar energy systems gather energy from sunlight. Active solar energy systems create electricity when sunlight shines on panels of silicon. Passive solar energy systems collect the heat of sunlight shining on a collector, which can be water or air or a simple wall. Wind energy systems gather energy as the blades or vanes of a windmill turn in the wind to run a water pump or an electric generator. Hydroelectric energy systems use the movement of water to turn an electric generator. Usually, the water is held behind a dam and is carefully released, but there are some turbines in rivers and tidal currents. All of these energy sources are considered alternatives to using fossil fuels and radioactive materials.

An alternative energy source does not use up a nonrenewable resource or create pollution when it generates power. Alternative energy sources are practical ways to make use of the energy freely available from the sun, wind, and water. But these alternative energy sources rely on the use of fossil fuels for mining and transportation. Metals and silicon are needed to make solar panels, windmills, and turbines. Great amounts of sand, gravel, and clay need to be moved to make dams. Eventually, most alternative energy sources need to be maintained or replaced. Many of the materials can be recycled or reused.

MORE THAN JUST FUEL

Fossil fuels like coal, natural gas, and petroleum are good for more than just fuel. These are complex mixtures of organic materials. Over time, they have been changed by heat and pressure into mixtures of substances that have many uses. Some of these substances have unique uses for industry, making crystals and chemicals.

As an eighteen-year-old research assistant experimenting with coal tar, William Henry Perkin (1838–1907) discovered aniline dye. It was a commercial success for Perkin and his employer.

If coal were used only as a fuel, no one would ever have discovered the many useful substances in it. One substance is aniline (also called phenylamine or aminobenzene). In 1856, William Henry Perkin was experimenting with coal, trying to discover a replacement for quinine, which is obtained from the bark of the cinchona tree and is used in medicines. Working with coal tar, he distilled out

This nuclear weapon test explosion took place in 1970 at Mururoa in French Polynesia. After 1974, nuclear tests were done underground to reduce radioactive poisoning downwind.

a substance that made a purple smear. He discovered the first artificial dye.

Perkin's search for a useful medicine in coal tar was a reasonable goal. Aniline is similar chemically to modern painkillers like acetaminophen and to sulfa drugs that cure infections. There are many kinds of medication and hospital supplies made from fossil fuels. When coal is being burned by the railway-car load in power plants, it's not just fuel that is burning. Electricity can be made in many ways, but some medicines and medical equipment can be made only from fossil fuels.

Radioactive materials are good for more than just running power plants. Doctors use radioactive materials for medical imaging in X-ray photographs, CAT scans, and PET scans. Radiation is also used to treat cancer. A few nuclear power plants are designed to create small amounts of materials for medical use. These irreplaceable materials are very radioactive for only a few hours.

OTHER NUCLEAR PRODUCTS

As the atomic pile or nuclear reactor was being invented, another use for radioactive material was being invented at the same time. Nuclear weapons bring together a critical mass of radioactive material without any carbon rods to slow down and control the reaction. The result is an explosion and scattering of radioactive particles. The force of the explosion is many times greater than for weapons made using fossil fuels. The United States used two nuclear weapons at the end of World War II (1939–1945) in Hiroshima and Nagasaki, Japan.

Many countries around the world, and the United Nations, are working hard to try to ensure that nuclear weapons are never used again in war. Part of this effort is the careful storage of spent nuclear fuel from nuclear reactors so that none of it is lost or stolen. The spent fuel can be used to make nuclear weapons.

WASTED ENERGY OPPORTUNITIES

Tens of thousands of oil wells produce hot water as well as crude oil. The water is usually between 250 and 300 degrees Fahrenheit (120–150 degrees Celsius). The hot water is considered a nuisance. It's usually salty. It has to be separated and dumped, adding about $4 per barrel to the cost of oil.

In 2002, Texas oil wells produced more than twelve billion barrels of hot water. The wasted energy in that hot water is the equivalent of the power produced by ten nuclear power plants, according to energy consultant Bernie Karl. In the book *Earth: The Sequel*, Karl is quoted as standing before a roomful of oil and utility executives on more than one occasion and telling them, "You should be ashamed."

Natural gas wells often have a flare or flame to burn gas that cannot be processed or sold. Sometimes, the flare burns off "sour gases," which are contaminants like hydrogen sulfide and carbon dioxide. Flaring gets rid of the explosive waste gas and reduces pollution. A flare makes the worksite safer, but it does not put the energy from burning the waste gas to any use.

Flaring is not just a temporary measure. Some flares near Edmonton in Canada have burned for thirty years or more. Gas companies almost never use the waste gas to generate heat or as an energy source. The waste gas is corrosive and ruins pipes.

Similar flares are sometimes necessary at garbage dumps and landfills. Explosive methane gas collects from rotting garbage. On occasion, the methane is burned in flares to get rid of it. A few landfills collect the methane and use it as fuel to burn garbage in an incinerator. The methane is "dirty fuel" with contaminants, but there is less pollution from the incinerator than from just letting the methane leak out of the landfill.

There are many opportunities to use energy instead of wasting it. In his book *The Coming Economic Collapse*, Stephen Leeb wrote of

Natural gas flares burn corrosive gases with a cooler flame than a high-temperature incinerator. The result is wasted heat from the flare and pollution that affects nearby people, animals, and plants.

cultural problems with nonrenewable resources. In many cultures around the world, people expect to use resources in the same ways that local people always have. But in India, China, and many African countries, some areas have been cleared almost entirely of trees. People need to walk for hours each day to find enough wood for fuel to cook a meal. In addition, globalization is bringing modern technology to developing nations. Some corporations expect to use resources and create pollution just as in Western and Communist nations.

Leeb calls these expectations "our psychological blind spots: conformity, authority, and groupthink." To Leeb, the biggest obstacle for people today is misplaced priorities. Wanting to own a car does not mean that an oil well's hot water has to be wasted. Wanting to build an electric power plant does not mean that the coal being burned has to make pollution.

MYTHS AND MYTHS AND FACTS
FACTS MYTHS AND
MYTHS MYTHS AND
FACTS
MYTHS AND MYTHS AND
FACTS
FACTS

MYTH: People always use up resources and find something new to use up.

FACT: People in many cultures around the world choose to live in a sustainable way within their environments. These cultures use resources in ways that are considerate of the ecology and the needs of future generations. Many aboriginal cultures have sustainable goals, as do the Mennonite, Hutterite, and Amish people of European descent.

MYTH: Somebody else will use up that resource, so it's my duty to get the benefit for my family.

FACT: Only the most greedy and selfish people benefit personally from resources that can be used to sustain a large number of people over a long period of time.

MYTH: New resources are accumulating just as they always have.

FACT: Minerals and metals, once mined, are irreplaceable. It takes millions of years for fossil fuel resources like petroleum to form by natural processes. Beds of gravel and clay accumulate during ice ages lasting thousands of years. Even a clear-cut forest needs two to four centuries before it might be possible to harvest fine old-growth timber.

CHAPTER ②

Products from Nonrenewable Resources

The use of natural resources in Western nations began to change after the Renaissance in western Europe, even before the Industrial Revolution. Businessmen and political leaders no longer thought of people as part of the natural world. It became traditional to view the world's resources and all nonhuman life as things for people to use. Natural resources were considered different from capital, which was a term for human-made goods and products.

A more modern approach to resource use is emerging. Economists now view many natural resources as forms of natural capital because they can be made better or worse by human action. The world's natural resources give living beings air and water, as well as food and shelter. The attitude that calls these resources natural capital recognizes that a healthy ecology has value to people. It's not enough just to

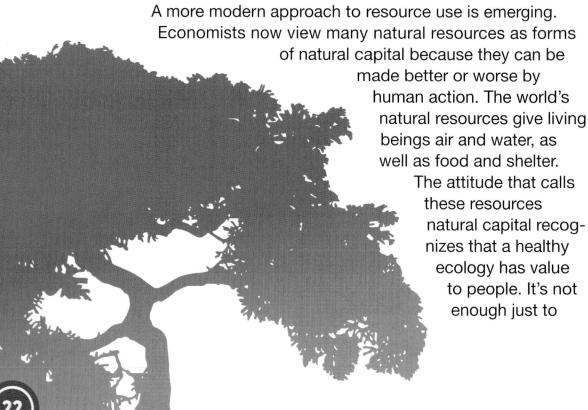

count the money that people earn by using a natural resource. When people are aware of any changes they are making to the ecology, they are considerate of its value.

RIGHTS OF NATURE

Ecuador is the first country to pass a law recognizing the rights of nature, which states: "Natural communities and ecosystems possess the unalienable right to exist, flourish, and evolve within Ecuador. Those rights shall be self-executing, and it shall be the duty and right of all Ecuadorian governments, communities, and individuals to enforce those rights." In plain talk, this means that the natural world is protected by law in Ecuador, and all citizens must enforce that law.

In most countries around the world, nature is treated as human property under the law. Except for Ecuador's laws, legal efforts to protect natural resources treat ecosystems as private property or common property. Until now, even the best environmental laws were all written under laws to benefit the human interests of property and commerce.

But it's not so odd to recognize the rights of nature. After all, some laws protect farm animals and pets. There are hunting laws to protect wild animals. Rare or endangered plants and animals are protected under state and federal laws. In Canada, many cities protect heritage trees (old-growth trees). New York State enacted the Bruce S. Kershner Heritage Tree Preservation and Protection Act in 2008 to protect old-growth trees on state land. Other U.S. states have proposed similar laws. Rights of nature in the constitution of a country can protect ecosystems and communities from projects that would ruin them. Ecuador's law means that local people and government agencies will make democratic decisions instead of letting corporations compete to exploit natural areas.

Since Ecuador passed a law recognizing the rights of nature, this strip mine in Rio Pastaza Canyon must operate with great consideration to sustain the natural life of the canyon.

WHERE ONE PRODUCT TAKES US: CLAY

Nonrenewable resources are not only energy sources. People use a variety of nonrenewable resources for making many products. For some products, it's very easy to tell what resources were used. Gold jewelry has a color different from other metals, for example. For other products, such as plastics, the petroleum resources used are not obvious.

One resource that most people don't realize is nonrenewable is clay. All of the clay in the world is formed by natural geological processes over hundreds of thousands—or millions—of years. Clay has many uses. Sometimes, it is an important ingredient in a product. For other products, clay is used to help process raw materials. Large quantities of china clay (also known as kaolin) are used when making cotton fibers into thread and weaving it into fabric. You may not be able to see clay in laundry products, pencils, or treated sewage, but it's there.

A use for clay that is not commonly known is the addition of clay as fillers. Clay fillers are used in a range of products. For agriculture, clay adds bulk to insecticides and makes nonstick coating for fertilizer pellets. Clay is an important part of many construction products, such as linoleum and cement, as well as paint and enamel. Toothpaste and cosmetics contain clay. Plastics like polypropylene and polyvinyl chloride (PVC) have clay added. Even flour sometimes has clay added.

There are three kinds of products where the clay content is most obvious or essential: pottery, bricks, and paper. Each of these products uses this nonrenewable resource for different purposes. These three products make good examples of how different planning is needed for each way that a nonrenewable resource is used.

POTTERY

People have used clay for pottery since Paleolithic times, for twenty thousand years or more in some parts of the world. When you think of

Park Güell in Barcelona, Spain, is full of fountains and constructions like this salamander sculpture that was designed and decorated by Antoni Gaudí from 1900 to 1914. Gaudí used broken pottery as decoration instead of throwing it in the garbage.

clay, you probably think of china dishes. Or perhaps you think of modeling clay for sculpting. Kaolin clay, or china clay, makes fine porcelain. In England alone, 1.1 million tons (about 1 million metric tons) of kaolin clay, or about one-third of the china clay used, goes into the making of fine porcelain each year.

For pottery, the clay is shaped and then fired by baking it in a hot oven called a kiln. Usually, the pottery is covered with a glaze made of water, clay, and powdered minerals. It is then fired again. Kilns can be fueled with wood, or fossil fuels, or powered with electricity. The temperatures reached are hot enough to melt glass and many metals.

Pottery is hard and brittle. Broken pottery pieces are sharp and have few uses. Spanish architect Antoni Gaudí was able to use broken pottery to make mosaics on several of his buildings. Pieces of broken pottery thousands of years old have turned up in old garbage in many places around the world.

BRICKS

The making of bricks and tiles for the construction industry is really a kind of pottery. But sculptures and dishes are not made from the same clay as bricks and floor tiles. The fine-grained white kaolin clay that makes good plates and figurines would be too hard and brittle for floor tiles or bricks. Instead, coarser clay is mixed with sand and powdered minerals. The resulting bricks and tiles are relatively softer than dishes but are more able to last under the stresses in a building. A brick is porous, almost like a sponge, compared with a bone china teacup.

Cheap, temporary bricks can be dried in sunshine in a hot climate. Some of these cheaper bricks have mud or cow dung mixed into the clay. But for buildings that will last, most bricks are fired in large industrial kilns. The fuel can be wood or charcoal. But in China, it is usually coal. The clay brick industry is a major source of air pollution

Brick buildings aren't all square and plain. Douglas Cardinal designed the Museum of the American Indian in Washington, D.C., making curves that change how people use the spaces in the building.

in developing countries. The United Nations (UN) and the International Energy Agency (IEA) are working to encourage all countries to control air pollution.

Another major source of air pollution in developing countries is the making of concrete and concrete bricks, which also contain clay. At least 1 ton (0.9 metric ton) of carbon dioxide gas is released for every ton of concrete made. The smoke from fossil fuels and carbon dioxide are greenhouse gases. These gases are believed by many scientists to be causing the earth's atmosphere to be warming up like a greenhouse and causing global climate change.

The photographs in these magazines are printed as clearly as they are because up to 30 percent of a glossy magazine is not paper. Instead, it is smooth white clay.

PAPERMAKING

Still more clay, usually kaolin, is used in papermaking. Paper is made with wood fibers that are cooked into pulp. Clay is mixed into the pulp to give strength and smoothness to many kinds of paper. Without clay, large paper mills would not be able to use machines to make paper. When clay is mixed into the wet slurry of wood fibers, the paper dries tough enough to wind in big rolls to be pulled through large printing presses. Clay also fills in gaps between fibers so that the paper is smooth. It's hard to print with ink on paper that has a rough texture like handmade paper.

NATURAL CAPITAL

How can someone measure the economy of a nation? It's not only the dollars earned and saved in banks. An economy is more than the money spent on capital like buildings and roads. The natural capital needs to be considered as well. A nation's economy is affected by how natural resources are being used and by ecological damage. The word "economy" is based on the Greek word *oikos*, for "household." A household needs more than a sturdy shelter and food. That is obvious when a forest fire or flood happens. A national economy shelters and feeds its citizens, using natural resources. The economy is affected by how the resources are used.

Clay is also used as a surface coating that is particularly good for glossy magazines. The result is a smooth surface that takes images well. But the high content of clay makes the glossy paper unrecyclable. Newsprint usually has about 8 percent clay, while magazines can contain up to 30 percent. Unrecycled paper will eventually compost in a garbage dump, but the clay is unrecoverable.

EACH RESOURCE AFFECTS OTHERS

It's an odd thought that when clay becomes scarce in a country, the cost of making paper will increase. There is just as much wood to make paper from, after all. But there are other questions to consider. There may not be enough railway cars to ship the needed clay, not without causing problems in shipping the country's grain harvests.

When any one nonrenewable resource runs out, the use of many other resources is affected. Mining metal ores would be done very slowly without the use of machines run on fossil fuels, for example. Some nonrenewable resources are abundant. Others are rare and prized, such as diamonds.

The use of a resource can have unexpected effects. When fuel is distilled from petroleum, there are a lot of waste products. From these discards, plastics and chemical fertilizers are made so that completely new industries have been created using these toxic wastes. But these materials have lasting bad effects in landfills and croplands, harming both human health and the environment.

It's hard to calculate the influence of a single industry within a nation's economy. The petroleum industry employs hundreds of thousands of U.S. workers, mostly in the Gulf states and Alaska. In addition, fossil fuels are essential for most industries. Engines run on fossil fuels are the backbone of transportation and the national economy. Nearly 80 percent of U.S. workers drive to work. Another 9 percent carpool, and most of the rest take public transportation, according to U.S. Census Bureau statistics quoted by the Center for American Progress.

CHAPTER 3

Lasting Effects of Consuming Nonrenewable Resources

Most business development happens at its own speed for its own reasons. Even community development is an effort to meet the needs of the community. From the point of view of many real estate developers or business owners, natural resources are something to be used. For them, nonrenewable resources are an opportunity, not a responsibility.

There are also people who take a longer view. Some planners consider what the needs of the community will be in ten years, fifty years, or more. Will there be any of the resources left then, or will only pollution be left? As workers grow older and retire, businesses need to be able to find new workers. When raw materials like marble are shipped to other countries, so are the jobs making marble countertops, rolling pins, and sculpture. People who live near a resource may end up with no

A nonrenewable resource like this carved argillite, a Haida raven totem, can be used locally for cultural reasons. Finished products sold to distant buyers bring more money to a community than raw materials can.

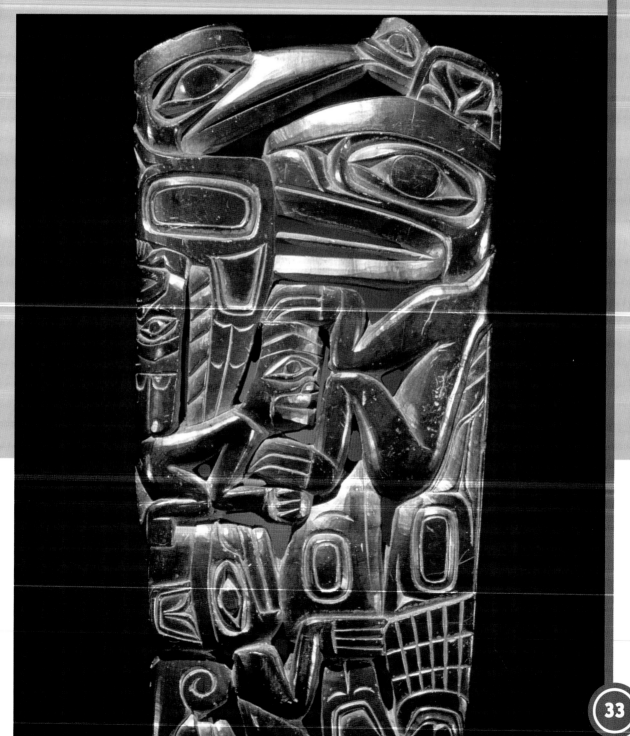

local work opportunities but may do rough physical labor sending raw materials to distant factories. It takes planning to decide how a community can benefit from processing local resources into useful products. It takes consideration to realize how large an area can be affected by resource use.

EXTRA OPPORTUNITIES

It can be hard at first to see that there is any choice other than using up an available resource as quickly as possible. Many people work at jobs where nonrenewable resources are gathered and shipped off to distant factories. Speed and efficiency are goals in this kind of work.

It's possible to find ways to use a resource without disturbing any more of the environment than necessary. Furthermore, nonrenewable resources provide more opportunities than only service jobs.

A good example of these opportunities is a black rock called argillite. It's found in Haida Gwaii, the Queen Charlotte Islands near the Alaskan panhandle. Haida artists turn argillite into carvings in both modern and traditional styles. Some of the Haida people could easily make a little income selling blocks of argillite from their quarry to rock collector shops across the United States and Canada. But they have decided not to sell uncarved argillite. Their works of art bring far more money to the community than the rough stones ever could. The stone still disappears from the quarry. But a lot happens before carvings leave Haida Gwaii. Artists teaching students their cultural traditions use the stone. Art dealers who market the carvings connect with galleries, museums, and universities to sell these and other works of art. Argillite carving is one part of the cultural renewal in Haida Gwaii. The local economy is supported, as are the traditions. The argillite is not being sold as quickly as possible in rough blocks for distant artists to carve and sell. The nonrenewable resource argillite is being used in a way that sustains the local community.

NUMBERS TO THINK ABOUT

The International Energy Agency (IEA) estimates that at the rate people used fossil fuels in 2008, there are possibly some forty years left of petroleum and gas. For coal, there are perhaps 165 years left. Many experts estimate there is far less. One of the effects of using these fossil fuels is the release of carbon into the atmosphere. By 2030, the IEA estimates that humans will have released approximately 1,000 gigatons (907 metric gigatons) of carbon. This is cause for alarm about global climate change. As of 2006, carbon emissions totaled about 300 gigatons (272 metric gigatons). The effects on local and global climates are disastrous and still being measured. The changes are being debated.

Sustainable development is the use of resources to meet the needs of the present, without compromising the ability of future generations to meet their own needs. Sustainable development balances the needs of society, the economy, and the environment.

GHOST TOWNS

There are ghost towns in various places across the United States. A ghost town is a rather eerie place, with empty buildings. Few or no people live where there were once dozens, or hundreds. One of the most common reasons for people to leave a town is that the resources they relied on when it was built simply aren't there anymore. It takes a

Burning fossil fuel makes dangerous wastes. A retaining pond at Kingston Fossil Plant in Harriman, Tennessee, spilled 1 billion gallons (4 billion liters) of coal ash slurry over nearby homes and waterways.

network of human activity to support a town. When all of a nonrenewable resource has gone from the town to a larger population center, the town may no longer be supported.

There are a string of ghost towns in the foothills of the Rocky Mountains, along the Brazeau River, where coal was mined in open pits from 1900 to 1960. Mercoal, Robb, and Coal Valley were fine villages with schools and doctors. Cadomin even had stores with women's fashions in 1918. When the coal that was cheap to mine was gone, there was no work. The railway line shut down. Most of the people left these small towns by the early 1960s. Only after 2001 did some developers promote the Coal Branch towns for recreational properties. Other ghost towns have come back from obscurity to be communities of artists and musicians.

ECOLOGICAL DAMAGE

When people use nonrenewable resources, there are effects on local ecology. Industry not only creates products that people want. Industrial byproducts are also made. Some of these byproducts are waste materials and garbage. Others are air and water pollution. It does people little good to have decent jobs at the mine and mill at their hometown making vermiculite out of asbestos fibers if the fibers sicken many people and farm animals nearby.

An entire biome—a local environment of plants and animals supported by soil, water, and air—can be changed by industry. More than one kind of plant or animal will suffer when a biome is damaged. Rare plants and animals become endangered or extinct. When people have made a gravel pit or a strip mine, local plants and animals can no longer live in that place.

When people dig out a gravel pit or a limestone quarry, the water drainage for the area is permanently changed. Even if later the topsoil is put back and new trees are planted, the local streams will drain differently on the surface and underground. The change might not look obvious. But that area might no longer be able to support some kinds of plants or the insects and animals that depend on them. The plants that can survive may be like kudzu, a fast-growing weed that chokes trees. The animals that move in may be rats that eat all of the local bird eggs. If there are no birds to eat mosquitoes, people may end up getting malaria from mosquito bites.

The actions of whales are not a mystery hidden in a vast, unknowable ocean. Whales live in the same waters that humans use. People's use of shared resources is crowding out and starving orcas.

People's health is harmed by pollution from factories, power plants, and transporting workers, causing heart and lung diseases and cancer. Wild animals are stressed by noisy people. Mines produce piles of waste rock called tailings; rainwater soaks metals and minerals out of tailings to poison streams. Oil wells spill crude oil onto farmers' fields. Burning fossil fuels puts pollution in the air and water. The oceans and atmosphere are warming, changing weather and natural habitats. Pollution is only one effect, but it is rarely temporary. It can permanently change an area's local ecology, or the entire planet.

USING UP RENEWABLE RESOURCES

Some resources renew themselves naturally, such as water or soil or wild fish. It is important for people to use those resources wisely, instead of using up everything available.

Water moves in a renewing cycle as rain falls from clouds, runs down streams, and evaporates into the air and becomes clouds again. But water is not a renewable resource when people misuse it. Since the 1960s, the Caspian Sea and the Aral Sea in Asia have shrunk to about half their former size. Water from two rivers is being diverted to grow cotton and for industry.

Water can become unusable for drinking or farming. Factory farms are hosed out with clean drinking water. The runoff is full of manure that contains germs like *E. coli* 0157:H7, a lethal version of a common germ. The runoff collects in streams, feeding so many algae that fish are smothered. The runoff can get into groundwater and infect people and animals that drink that water.

People can even take water permanently out of the water cycle. Water is injected deep underground into petroleum domes to maintain pressure in oil wells. The water will never come back to the surface and become rain again.

Dirt may seem to be everywhere underfoot. But not all dirt is good for growing plants. When forests are clear-cut, the topsoil may wash away in rainstorms. It takes hundreds of years for new soil to form. If people raise crops without letting farm soil recover, the soil will be less productive. The clear-cutting of forests and overgrazing created the deserts in Lebanon, northern Algeria, and Morocco.

People spend vast resources mining rare diamonds for industrial use and jewelry. The most precious things in the world are beautiful and irreplaceable because they are useful and sustain life.

Oceans look huge and seem to have many fish. But people have taken many salmon from the Pacific coast near Washington State and Alaska. There are so few salmon left that in 2008 the orcas near Seattle were becoming thin. It's hard for these whales to catch salmon when the Strait of Juan de Fuca has become the world's second-busiest waterway. There's a lot of noise and traffic from hundreds of large ships and small boats. Biologists see this traffic affecting both the fish and the whales. Seven adult whales died and one baby was born in 2008, leaving only eighty-three resident orcas living in that area. Moreover, commercial fishermen report that the salmon harvest is lower every year.

When people use resources without thinking about the results, many unexpected changes can happen. Even so-called renewable resources can be used in a way and at a rate that do not allow for natural renewal. These resources are then revealed as nonrenewable resources.

HOTELLING'S RULE: EXPLOITING A RESOURCE WILL RAISE ITS PRICE

It's easy to know the price paid for fuel oil pumped into a tank, ready to fuel a furnace. It's not hard to figure out what part of the price went to pay the trucker's wages. But the value of the crude oil before it was refined, and who (if anyone) owns that value, is harder to determine. Economists call the value of work and the goods people make capital. Economist Harold Hotelling named some of the values of a natural resource.

In a 1931 article on nonrenewable resource management, Hotelling showed that using up a resource makes it scarcer and increases its price. The maximum price for a resource being exploited is known as Hotelling rent, or scarcity rent.

Scarcity rent is a kind of profit that economists call a resource rent. It is income made not by work but by access to the resource.

Using the term "resource rent" is a way that economists recognize natural capital. Natural resources have value that is separate from the work people do.

HARTWICK'S RULE: INVEST RESOURCE RENTS

A person who works should get the income that he or she earns. A person who starts a business should get the income from the business after paying his or her workers. But it's not so clear who should get the profit from using a natural resource. Because nonrenewable resources can be used up, it's important to spend wisely the profit earned by using these resources.

A nation must invest net income from nonrenewable resources in capital to improve its infrastructure, wrote economist John M. Hartwick in 1977. The improvement in lasting buildings, roads, and universities will remain, even as the resource is used up.

Hartwick's rule is being put into use by many nations around the world. The Alaska Permanent Fund was created in 1976 so that the state could invest 25 percent of the proceeds from sales of mineral rights like oil and gas. The province of Alberta in Canada created the Heritage Fund in 1970 and contributes a portion of the provincial oil revenues to it. Iceland has a similar fund of its own, but its oil revenues are earned at a higher price per barrel of oil extracted.

TEN GREAT QUESTIONS TO ASK A SCIENCE TEACHER

 How will a nature reserve or national park protect resources as well as biomes?

 How is this electrical power generated?

 Is this product made by using any recycled materials?

 What is this product's environmental footprint?

 How many years' worth of resources are available for making this product in the future?

 How is the natural capital from this product being spent?

 What community development programs does this product's manufacturer maintain?

 What renewable resource alternatives are used when making this product and in the manufacturer's facilities in general?

 What kind of vehicles are in the manufacturer's transportation fleet, and are these vehicles powered by fossil fuels or alternatives?

 Does this manufacturer transport materials overseas by boat or by airplane?

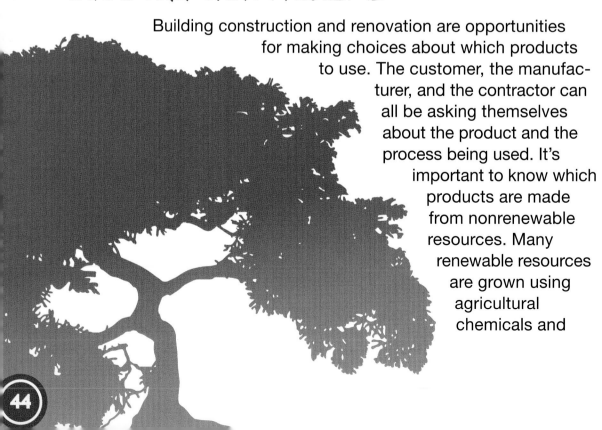

CHAPTER ④

Making Choices About Nonrenewable Resources

Just because a product is made from materials that are renewable resources does not mean that the product itself is "green," or an environmentally sensible choice. Making the decision of which product to use in a home or work environment can be tricky. There may be factors to think about in ways that are not immediately obvious.

CARPETING OVER PROBLEMS

Building construction and renovation are opportunities for making choices about which products to use. The customer, the manufacturer, and the contractor can all be asking themselves about the product and the process being used. It's important to know which products are made from nonrenewable resources. Many renewable resources are grown using agricultural chemicals and

Jute grows quickly, making inexpensive and organic natural fiber. This natural fiber has been used and composted for thousands of years before fibers were ever made from petroleum waste products.

a lot of fossil fuel for farm equipment and transportation. If the material of a carpet, for example, is made from renewable jute fiber, that's a good start. The jute could be grown organically without using chemicals. It could also be grown near the factory instead of being shipped overseas.

Ray Anderson is the owner of Interface, a U.S. company that has made carpets since 1976. He was inspired to change his company's methods in 1993. Anderson believed that business "would become more

The first Veggie Pride Parade took place in the Meatpacking District in New York City on May 18, 2008. Vegetarian food uses far less water and tractor fuel than that needed to raise meat.

profitable by reducing waste and energy use and its overall impact on the planet," he was quoted as saying in *Earth: The Sequel*, a book by Fred Krupp. "I realized that the way I'd been running my company had been the way of the plunderer."

Anderson's company has reduced water pollution and fossil fuel use. It no longer prints patterns in dyes onto carpet tiles. The machines use loops of yarn to create carpet patterns instead, employing much less water and energy. Their top-selling product mimics the random disorder of a forest floor. There is no pattern to match when laying these carpet tiles, so there is less waste when it is installed. Worn tiles can be replaced without having to tear out an entire carpet. The results inspire Interface's employees and rivals. Greenhouse gas emission for the company has been reduced by 56 percent, while sales have increased by 49 percent.

John Gillespie is a materials expert, landscape designer, and horticulturalist. He said, "One of the keys to building green is getting the design and materials site-specific," according to Tyree Bridge in *BC Homes Magazine*. A good choice for a building on the Atlantic coast might not be as good for a

Vehicles that use electricity and alternative fuels instead of gasoline are now widely available. These vehicles, such as the extended-range electric Chevrolet Volt, are promoted as not only practical and useful but also fashionable, desirable, and socially responsible.

building on the Pacific coast. Gillespie ordered a batch of wool carpet for a house in Vancouver. Wool carpet is made from a renewable resource, sheep's wool. But the raw fleece was shipped from New Zealand to Greece to be spun and woven. The carpet was shipped through England to a Canadian seaport in Halifax, Nova Scotia. From there, the carpet was trucked to Vancouver. "When I figured out the mileage on that carpet, I couldn't believe it," Gillespie said. He was upset by how much fossil fuel was used to transport the wool carpet. "In terms of green, it would have been better to just order something from back east."

MAKING YOUR OWN GOOD CHOICES

There are many choices you can make about your own use of nonrenewable resources. What you eat, what transportation you use, how you furnish your room—you may have more choices than you think at first.

Because plants and animals grow naturally, food should be a renewable resource. But most food these days is grown and shipped with the use of fossil fuels. A vegetarian diet uses far fewer fossil fuels than are needed to raise animals for meat. As Alisa Smith and James MacKinnon wrote in their book *Plenty*, the food that Americans and Canadians eat now typically travels between 1,500 and 3,000 miles (2,414–4,828 kilometers) from farm to plate. When they learned this statistic, Smith and MacKinnon ate food grown within 100 miles (161 km) of their home for a year.

Their book became a best seller. The "hundred mile diet" has now become a fun and fashionable way to learn about locally grown food. If not for a year, then for a party or for one day every week, many people are choosing to eat food that has not been transported any farther than 100 miles.

There are more ways to get around town than by owning a gasoline-powered car. A bicycle is made of much less metal than a car and rolls without fuel. For many people, a bike meets most of their transportation

A modern product label, such as the one pictured here and used by a British-based international grocery chain, carries information that describes the resources used to make the product. A product's carbon footprint is the amount of carbon dioxide that is released into the atmosphere in creating the product and getting it to the supermarket shelf.

Buy 3 for £4

Long Term Price Offer

TESCO Orange Smooth

NOT FROM CONCENTRATE

...cked...
...processe...
within
24 hours

working with the Carbon Trust

360g CO2

The carbon footprint of this juice is 360g per 250ml serving and we have committed to reduce it

By comparison the footprint of Tesco Long-Life Pure Orange Juice is 240g per 250ml serving, which is lower because less energy is required to chill ...transport ...juice

Any 3 for £2.25 £

working with the Carbon Trust

260g CO2
Compared to pure squeezed juice
360g

per 250ml serving

The carbon footprint of this juice is 260g per 250ml serving and we have committed to reduce it

By comparison the footprint of Tesco 100% Pure Squeezed Orange Juice is 360g per 250ml serving, which is higher because more energy is required to chill and transport 100% pure juice than concentrated juice

needs. Riding the bus is an alternative that shares the use of fossil fuel among more people. A car-share cooperative lets a group of people share the use of a few cars when needed.

There are other options for cars as well, such as the two-seater Smart Car. The IEA estimates that by 2050, as much as 30 percent of the fuel used for transportation could be biofuel from plants instead of fossil fuels. General Motors (GM) is one of the companies that is developing alternative fuel strategies. GM's Chevy Volt is an electric car with a gasoline engine (or a diesel engine or hydrogen engine) to use when the batteries run out of electricity. The company is also working to produce ethanol fuel from waste products instead of from corn.

As for furnishing your room or home, there are many choices. Are there any products made by local companies using renewable resources? Perhaps you'll be able to choose a mattress made of latex from rubber trees. A futon made of organic cotton may suit you better. An old bed frame or desk doesn't have to be thrown away. Try a few tightened screws and a little brass polish, wood stain, or paint. You might give old furniture some vintage style or make a personal piece of modern art.

CONSUMER ATTITUDES

There was a popular saying when rationing of consumer goods was in place during World War II: "Use it up, wear it out, make it do, or do without." At that time, people couldn't just buy another coat or car or nylon stockings. That attitude doesn't seem old-fashioned in the twenty-first century. It's beginning to become popular again.

The marketing of consumer goods doesn't account for the cost of using up nonrenewable resources. Price tags don't say what part of the price for a product goes to pay for nonrenewable resources. As venture capitalist John Doerr said in *Earth: The Sequel*, "It's really hard to change consumer behavior when consumers don't know how much their behavior costs."

APPLYING WHAT YOU KNOW

When you consider your personal use of nonrenewable resources, it's not enough just to choose to use products made from renewable resources. Don't forget about how products are made available to you, trucked in to stores. Remember that your nation is building an entire infrastructure of services for your benefit. There are hospitals, roads, schools, and communications. As a citizen, you have a duty to participate in the decisions that sustain this infrastructure. It is possible for people to use nonrenewable resources carefully and responsibly.

All products used in the United States have ingredient lists and company records. This is so you will know what you are using and how it was made. Read labels. Ask questions when you go into a business. And do Internet searches among company Web sites. You can find out if the products you want to use are made using nonrenewable resources in a responsible manner.

When you choose to consume nonrenewable resources, do so mindfully. Know where the products you use come from and how they are transported to you. Learn what you can about how the infrastructure of the United States uses up resources at a rate that cannot be sustained. A good way to start is by learning how nonrenewable resources are consumed to make and distribute consumer goods. Then, take that experience to the decisions you make about essential things like food staples, shelter, energy use, and transportation. There is no one right answer for how nonrenewable resources ought to be used. There are plenty of reasons for any of the decisions you may choose to make.

Even young people can become informed and prepared for making active decisions in all of these areas. When you work toward a career or start a business of your own, that's an opportunity to apply what you know about nonrenewable resources.

biome An ecological environment, including plants, animals, water, atmosphere, soil, and minerals.

capital Product of human work, usually a lasting object with reliable value.

conformity The action of doing things the same way that other people do.

contaminants Unwanted substances, sometimes dangerous or poisonous, such as hydrogen sulfide mixed into natural gas.

corrosive Being worn away slowly by a chemical reaction.

critical mass An amount of radioactive element that releases enough particles to cause a chain reaction that can be sustained.

ecology The study of interactions of organisms with each other and their environment.

exploit To make efficient use of something or someone; to take unfair advantage of a person or situation for one's own purposes.

greenhouse gas Gas like carbon dioxide and pollution from burning fossil fuels, which are believed to cause global climate change.

groupthink The effort that people make as a group to try to think the same way for good or bad reasons; a word made up by George Orwell in his book *1984*.

Hartwick's rule Invest resource rent, or using the net income from nonrenewable resources to invest in lasting improvements in national infrastructure.

Hotelling rent The maximum net price that can be obtained during the full extraction of a nonrenewable resource; also known as scarcity rent.

infrastructure A nation's lasting capital, including buildings, roads, utilities, schools and universities, health care, and justice systems.

natural capital The value of a natural resource, particularly a nonre-newable resource; the net profit from the sale of a product after subtracting production costs and fair value for investment.

organic Relating to material made of or by living organisms or once-living organisms.

sustainable development The use of resources to meet the needs of the present, without compromising the ability of future generations to meet their own needs.

Christian Science Monitor
Environment: Bright Green Blog
210 Massachusetts Avenue
Boston, MA 02115
(617) 450-7929
Web site: http://features.csmonitor.com/environment
The *Christian Science Monitor* is a daily online newspaper that maintains a multimedia Web site, including a daily updated page on environmental concerns.

Community Environmental Legal Defense Fund (CELDF)
675 Mower Road
Chambersburg, PA 17202
(717) 709-0457
Web site: http://www.celdf.org
The CELDF was formed to provide free and affordable legal services to community-based groups and local governments working to protect their quality of life and the natural environment through building sustainable communities.

Energy Information Administration
1000 Independence Avenue SW
Washington, DC 20585
(202) 586-8800
Web site: http://www.eia.doe.gov
This office serves adults, students, and schoolchildren, providing information on energy data and statistics, in person, online, and by phone. There is a live expert available from 9 AM to 5 PM, Eastern Standard Time, from Monday to Friday.

Oracle ThinkQuest Education Foundation
North America contact: Denise Hobbs
(505) 255-2219
Web site: http://library.thinkquest.org/17940/index.html
The Oracle Foundation maintains ThinkQuest as an online library
of articles developed by students for students to use when
understanding many topics. The articles in the section "Atomic
Alchemy: Nuclear Processes" by team 17940 discuss atomic
energy and nuclear science, and are particularly useful and
well-illustrated with photographs.

Sustainable Development Indicators (SDI)
NASA Headquarters, Suite 5K39
Washington, DC 20546-0001
Web site: http://www.hq.nasa.gov/iwgsdi/Welcome.html
The SDI is one of the centers run by the National Aeronautics and
Space Administration (NASA). Through this Web site and other
NASA links, there is information about energy use and sustainable
use of nonrenewable resources.

United Nations Department of Economic and Social Affairs
Division for Sustainable Development
Two United Nations Plaza, Room DC2-2220
New York, NY 10017
(917) 367-3269
Web site: http://www.un.org/esa/sustdev/index.html
The international organization provides leadership and expertise in
sustainable development and monitors program progress.

U.S. Environmental Protection Agency (EPA)
Ariel Rios Building
1200 Pennsylvania Avenue NW
Washington, DC 20460
(202) 272-0167
Web site: http://www.epa.gov
The EPA writes regulations to enforce environmental laws written by
    Congress. It has ten regional offices serving each area of the
    United States to explain regulations and give grants to programs
    by schools, nonprofit groups, and state projects.

WEB SITES

Due to the changing nature of Internet links, Rosen Publishing has
developed an online list of Web sites related to the subject of this book.
This site is updated regularly. Please use this link to access the list:

http://www.rosenlinks.com/gre/nonr

FOR FURTHER READING

Barnes, Peter. *Climate Solutions: What Works, What Doesn't, and Why: A Citizen's Guide*. White River Junction, VT: Chelsea Green Publishing, 2008.

Black, Edwin. *Internal Combustion: How Corporations and Governments Addicted the World to Oil and Derailed the Alternatives*. New York, NY: St. Martin's Press, 2008.

McQuaig, Linda. *It's the Crude, Dude: War, Big Oil, and the Fight for the Planet*. Toronto, Ontario: Doubleday Canada, 2004.

Morgan, Sally. *The Pros and Cons of Coal, Gas, and Oil* (The Energy Debate). New York, NY: Rosen Publishing, 2008.

Morris, Neil. *Fossil Fuels: Energy Sources*. North Mankato, MN: Smart Apple Media, 2007.

Pfeiffer, Dale Allen. *Eating Fossil Fuels: Oil, Food, and the Coming Crisis in Agriculture*. Gabriola, British Columbia: New Society Publishers, 2006.

Schlager, Neil, and Jayne Weisblatt, eds. *Alternative Energy, Volumes 1, 2, and 3*. Detroit, MI: UXL, Thomson, Gale. 2006.

Spilsbury, Richard, and Louise Spilsbury. *The Earth's Resources*. New York, NY: Chelsea House Publishers, 2006.

ThinkQuest. "Nuclear Waste Storage." Retrieved October 20, 2008 (http://library.thinkquest.org/17940/texts/nuclear_waste_storage/ nuclear_waste_storage.html).

Alaska Permanent Fund Corporation. "What Is the Alaska Permanent Fund?" Retrieved October 17, 2008 (http://www.apfc.org/home/Content/permFund/aboutPermFund.cfm).

Asheim, Geir B., Wolfgang Buchholtz, John M. Hartwick, Tapan Mitra, and Cees Withagen. "Constant Saving Rates and Quasi-arithmetic Population Growth Under Exhaustible Resource Constraints." *Journal of Environmental Economics and Management*, 53, 2007, pp. 213–239.

Bakan, Joel. *The Corporation: The Pathological Pursuit of Profit and Power*. New York, NY: Free Press, 2004.

Booth, David. "U.S. Giants See Profit in Eco-friendly Autos." *Victoria Times-Colonist*, November 5, 2008, p. B7.

Bridge, Tyee. "The Right Stuff." *BC Homes Magazine*. September/October 2008, pp. 27–28.

Brune, Michael. *Coming Clean: Breaking America's Addiction to Oil and Coal*. San Francisco, CA: Sierra Club Books, 2008.

Caliber Planning. "What Is Flaring?" Retrieved October 28, 2008 (https://www.proactiver-fn.com/index.php?content=faq&section=flaring).

Curie, Marie. "Radium and Radioactivity." *Century Magazine*, 1904. American Institute of Physics. Retrieved November 1, 2008 (http://www.aip.org/history/curie/article.htm).

Dormer, Wolfgang. "BP's Perspective on Future Fuels." March 18, 2008. Retrieved October 20, 2008 (http://www.mam.gov.tr/eng/institutes/ee/cnapril2008/sunu/bp.ppt).

Energy Information Administration. "Petroleum Basic Statistics." September 2008. Retrieved October 15, 2008 (http://www.eia.doe.gov/basics/quickoil.html).

Gold, Thomas. *The Deep Hot Biosphere: The Myth of Fossil Fuels*. New York, NY: Copernicus Books, 2001.

Graham, Ian. *Fossil Fuels: A Resource Our World Depends On*. Chicago, IL: Heinemann Library, 2005.

Hartwick, John M. "Intergenerational Equity and the Investment of Rents from Exhaustible Resources." *American Economic Review*, 67, December 1977, pp. 972–4.

Herbert, John W. "BC's Orcas Suffer Their Worst Die-off in a Decade." *Kayak Yak*, October 26, 2008. Retrieved October 26, 2008 (http://kayakyak.blogspot.com).

Jaccard, Mark Kenneth. *Sustainable Fossil Fuels: The Unusual Suspect in the Quest for Clean and Enduring Energy*. Cambridge. MA: Cambridge University Press, 2005.

Krupp, Fred, and Miriam Horn. *Earth: The Sequel. The Race to Reinvent Energy and Stop Global Warming*. New York, NY: W. W. Norton & Co., 2008.

Leeb, Stephen, with Glen Strathy. *The Coming Economic Collapse: How You Can Thrive When Oil Costs $200 a Barrel*. New York, NY: Warner Business, 2006.

Morgan, James. "Mud Eruption 'Caused by Drilling.'" BBC News, November 1, 2008. Retrieved November 1, 2008 (http://news.bbc.co.uk/2/hi/science/nature/7699672.stm).

O'Carroll, Eoin. "Ecuador Constitution Would Grant Inalienable Rights to Nature." Christian Science Monitor's Bright Green Blog, September 3, 2008. Retrieved October 15, 2008 (http://features.csmonitor.com/environment/2008/09/03/ecuador-constitution-would-grant-inalienable-rights-to-nature).

Parker, Janine. "The Electron Centennial Page." Retrieved November 1, 2008 (http://www.davidparker.com/janine/electron.html).

Smith, Alisa, and James MacKinnon. *Plenty: One Man, One Woman, and a Raucous Year of Eating Locally*. New York, NY: Random House, 2007.

Tomko, Heather. "Ecuador's Constitutional Amendment Will Benefit Environment." *The Tartan*, October 13, 2008. Retrieved October 17, 2008 (http://www.thetartan.org/2008/10/13/forum/ecuador).

Waters, Bella. *Kazakhstan in Pictures*. Minneapolis, MN: Twenty-First Century Books, 2007.

Weller, Christian E. "Record Gas Prices Add Pressure to Already Squeezed Consumers." Center for American Progress, April 22, 2008. Retrieved October 14, 2008 (http://www.americanprogress.org/issues/2008/04/record_gas_prices.html).

INDEX

ABOUT THE AUTHOR

For fifteen years, Paula Johanson operated an organic-method market garden, selling produce and sheep's wool at farmer's markets. She has written and edited more than twenty nonfiction books on science, health, and literature. At two or more conferences each year, she leads panel discussions on practical science and how it applies to home life and creative work. An accredited teacher, Johanson has written and edited curriculum educational materials for the Alberta Distance Learning Centre in Canada.

PHOTO CREDITS

Cover, p. 1 © www.istockphoto.com/Michael Utech; p. 7 Melanie Stetson Freeman/Christian Science Monitor/Getty Images; pp. 8–9 © George Steinmetz/Corbis; p. 10 © www.istockphoto.com/Sherwin McGehee; p. 12 Maxim Kniazkov/AFP/Getty Images; p. 15 Wikipedia; p. 16 AFP/Getty Images; p. 19 © Benjamin Lowy/Corbis; p. 24 © Alison Wright/Corbis; p. 26 © www.istockphoto.com/Carri Keill; p. 28 Wikimedia Commons; p. 29 Don Emmert/AFP/Getty Images; p. 33 © Boltin Picture Library/Bridgeman Art Library; pp. 36, 50 © AP Images; pp. 38–39 © www.istockphoto.com/Frank Leung; p. 40 Carl De Souza/AFP/Getty Images; p. 45 © Rupak De Chowdhuri/Reuters/Corbis; pp. 46–47 lrphotos/Newscom.com; p. 48 Jacky Naegelen/Reuters/Newscom.com.

Designer: Nicole Russo; Editor: Kathy Kuhtz Campbell;
Photo Researcher: Amy Feinberg

Mission San Fernando